Pitchersize

Working Out The Perfect PITCH

I *love* this book! For years, before I became an author and speaker, I worked in newspaper publishing and advertising sales. Dean's concept of the pitch—connecting the elusive worlds of Vision, Worth, Perfectionism, and Relationships— is amazing. This may not have been the book that Dean sat down to write, but it is definitely the book he was *meant* to write!

—Gerry Gavin, best-selling Hay House author of *If You Could Talk to an Angel* and *Messages from Margaret* and weekly radio host
(www.gerrygavin.com)

This hands-on book and its practical advice will help you to deeply understand the philosophy of the pitch phenomenon and how to survive in the early stages of entrepreneurship. This book will also boost the spirit of those result-oriented individuals who have the idea to sell or the start-up company to run.

—Kari Juhala, senior lecturer,
Turku University of Applied Sciences

I really do like that the book, *Pitchersize*, is as outspoken as its author, Dean DiNardi. DiNardi gives straight and honest feedback without mincing words. And still he is genuinely interested in helping, very supportive, and has a great sense of humor (in the book and personally). The book *Pitchersize* is really motivating, easy to read and to understand, and a perfect ancillary for pitching, that you can always scan back on and be reminded about the tools to use for a perfect pitch.

—Lina Toivonen, owner, Smooth it

Pitchersize

Working Out The Perfect PITCH

And Some Characteristics of Being an Entrepreneur

Dean A. DiNardi

BALBOA.
PRESS

A DIVISION OF HAY HOUSE

Balboa Press books may be ordered through booksellers or by contacting:

Balboa Press
A Division of Hay House
1663 Liberty Drive
Bloomington, IN 47403
www.balboapress.com
1 (877) 407-4847

Print information available on the last page.

ISBN: 978-1-5043-6880-3 (sc)
ISBN: 978-1-5043-6881-0 (hc)
ISBN: 978-1-5043-6882-7 (e)

Library of Congress Control Number: 2016918634

Balboa Press rev. date: 09/04/2019

Contents

Acknowledgments vii

Introduction..ix

The Pitch and Verbal Marketing 1

Chapter 1 What Is the Pitch? 3

Brainchild.. 17

Chapter 2 Vision 19

Goals...29

Chapter 3 Mapping 31

Willingness 45

Chapter 4 What's It Worth? 47

Perfectionism 57

Chapter 5 Overcoming Perfectionism.................59

Relationships 67

Chapter 6 It's All About Relationships 69

Connection 77

Chapter 7 Connecting....................................... 79

Turbocharge your Pitch 85

Chapter 8 Pitching on Steroids........................ 87

   Presence...89

Professionalism 92

Pizzazz 93

Afterword...97

About the Author 99

Pitch Deck 103

Acknowledgments

To all the people in the world who have ever wanted to do something but felt too old, felt the time was never right, felt they didn't have enough education or experience or money …

To all the people who have taken the time to read this book and to those who found value in it and applied it and succeeded by it. To all those who have succeeded in life and shared their knowledge, wisdom, and experiences with those seeking guidance.

To all the people who helped me get started by offering their knowledge, experience, and insight on how to write books and build businesses, including the Turku Science Park, the people at Spark-up, Donna Kozik (MYBIGBUSINESSCARD.com), and Chris Curran (author of *Leap Beyond Your Limits*).

To old friends Ted Banta and Jimmy Demestre, who reminded me I have what it takes and keep on supporting me in all the endeavors I embark on in my life. A special thanks to Gerry Gavin, a friend and the author of *Messages from Margaret* and *If You Could Talk to an Angel*.

To my parents, brothers, sisters, and extended family for supporting me. Family is a blessing—often in disguise until one learns to unmask oneself.

To my wife, daughter, and son—they were my biggest reason (my why) for succeeding and striving beyond my comfort zone and false perception of limitedness. I strive to be the example for them, my children, to succeed by in their personal life and in business.

To God for providing the energy, space, and environment for anything to be possible. And to my faith, even if it is hidden at times, because without it I might not have known it was possible.

Introduction
The Lineup

My son is now an "entrepreneur." That's what you're called when you don't have a job.

—*Ted Turner*

You want to pitch your product or service—your brainchild? You want to be an entrepreneur? Awesome! You have taken the first steps in an amazing life direction.

I want to make one point about being an entrepreneur before we begin: it's not a thing. It's more like a way of being, thinking, and doing. It's a way of life.

I had my first business at the age of ten. I was a professional clown doing all sorts of parties and events. Laugh if you must, but I got paid nicely by it. After that, no matter what I got into in my personal life - sports, meditation, yoga, acting, writing – I would look for ways to capitalize on it and turn a hobby, interest or passion into a paycheck. Offering something and receiving from it was a win-win. I never really developed any of them to serve as passive income or a sellable company, mostly because I was still dependent on the family business, and didn't have the courage to completely break free.

My family business was a good fundamental incubating atmosphere for me, ingraining an entrepreneur mind-set. Yet although it was an entrepreneurial environment, I was still working nine to five and didn't have enough control over implementing my vision. This fueled the already burning desire to create my own *something*, which eventually burned so hot that it propelled me to the next step of getting out on my own.

Through the years, I had learned that although the seed of entrepreneurialism was in my DNA, that didn't guarantee anything. It is up to, me, the individual to water that seed. What was going to water that seed for me? What was going to be the food for the growth to actualize this life?

I had to work hard and keep pushing against my perceived limitations and what I thought was possible or not. I needed a strong reason, a *why*, to forge ahead into the unknown.

Your *why* is something that is very important to you. It's something you find when you auger deep down inside of your gut and find that thing that means so much to you. You would find anything to have, do, accomplish, see it happen... Like making sure your lids don't go hungry.

Initially, after I started my first few ventures like a yoga studio with a friend, flipping real-estate properties, personal life coaching and seminar business I realized there was something missing. I didn't have a strong enough Why. I didn't have enough passion, motivation or drive to make them long lasting ventures.

Entrepreneurs have a Mindset that says they can and will, so they do. Many don't think about it or even consider it something other than normal thinking, however it is a unique way of thinking. Some naturally have it and it exists and develops as they breathe, some know it's there and actively develop and tune it, while others work hard to overcome old ways mindsets and actively develop this success mindset.

I mentioned earlier that I had the seed of Entrepreneurship in my DNA (natural mindset), however I had to water that seed and help it to grow. You must nurture and tend to this success mindset because it isn't the primary way of thinking in society. You will be met with opposition and adversity; you can't give in – you must intuitively know any other way is not a success way.

The good news is that the Success Mindset is learnable. A mindset is a mind set on a set of beliefs. You must change your belief system to change what your mind is set on. And even though I had been raised in a family of entrepreneurs and had always believed I can do anything, and it would always work out, just a question of what or how, there where beliefs I had to change. Identifying the sabotaging beliefs verses the success beliefs is the key and it's a personal growth process as well as a business one.

I realized that since I was still at the family firm and under the umbrella of safety and comfort, these ventures were hobbies—not quite my passion enough to get me to leave that safe space. I hadn't found my true and strong enough *why*. Yet I was slowly building my entrepreneurial muscles, one venture at a time.

I learned that when you do decide on something, a strong *why* is the thing that will push you off the ledge of comfort and uncertainty to really succeed. Whether it lasts forever or not isn't what matters, rather what you gain by it (money, knowledge, experience, connections).

I had always planned to write a book and actually started one several years ago. Then over the summer, I decided to hunker down and finish it. Unexpectedly, I found myself shipping this book off to the publisher in its place. The result of a stronger *why* and needed undertaking (opportunity).

Entrepreneurs see opportunity when it knocks and are able to push through doors to make it work. They are the catalysts to see it into existence, and they cultivate the courage, tenacity, and resources needed to capitalize on it. Though they often take chances and risks, these are calculated to the best degree possible. The rest is an inner knowing from experience and self-trust.

Being an entrepreneur is a personal, intimate, and tricky endeavor. I'm not sure anyone can actually be an expert on it. For me, it seems to be a constant learning experience and an evolving way of life. With that said, I am going to tell you how I see it and how it works for me, through my experience in the traditional workforce and the entrepreneurial world. Having found both rewarding, I can say that it truly depends on what you want for yourself and your life.

There are pros and cons to being an entrepreneur. Some people are made for this sort of life and some are not. However, even though anyone can learn how to be an entrepreneur, not everyone is made for. It's just like being a lawyer, a mechanic, an astronaut, or an actor—learning it doesn't mean your made for it. Nonetheless, it's worth the experience of trying.

Pitchersize started out as a book solely on the legendary elevator pitch that has evolved in the twenty-first century with the boom of start-up business ventures. The pitch has become somewhat of a celebrity as a popular way of getting a business recognized, getting funding, finding team members, and courting customers. Yet it's also been portrayed as sort of an evil villain because so many don't like to present or speak publicly.

It seemed to me that a book only on pitching would be somewhat short-chaptered and more like a book on acting in too many respects. That would cut the legs of the pitch out from under it. The pitch has so many more features to it than just standing up there and telling your idea and hoping for desired results. So I am going to offer you a great deal of information not only on the pitch and how to construct it and present it, but also on the mind-set behind it.

The quote above by Ted Turner about an entrepreneur being someone without a job is funny and scary at the same time. Ted Turner is a multibillionaire, with an estimated worth of $2.2 billion. And I'm sure his son doesn't need to work, or doesn't have to look far to find a job.

I'm going to suggest that Turner is actually referring to the underlying joke in the entrepreneur world—that when you do what you love, it's not a job. We might not have "jobs," but we have plenty of work that takes more than the time to do just a job.

Ted Turner wasn't always a billionaire. It was his tenacity that made him a billionaire as an entrepreneur. Which brings me to a quote by Gautam Adani, an Indian business tycoon whose estimated worth is $7 billion: "Being an entrepreneur is my dream job, as it tests one's tenacity." *Tenacity* means a firm grip on the desire to see something through—firmness or determination.

Gautam decided to leave his father's textile business and go out on his own. With just a few rupees in his pocket, he set out. Starting out as a diamond sorter, he moved along and eventually amassed a corporation involved in coal trading, ports, oil and gas exploration, and generators, to name a few areas. Ted Turner, on the other hand, started out in his father's advertising company and eventually went on to build the largest cable network in the world. He is well known for founding CNN and many other cable networks.

As for myself, I was part of a family business too—a multi-company corporation worth an estimated couple hundred million. We were not quite billionaires, but not too shabby. I decided to leave the business and move abroad with my wife and two children.

When I moved, I basically took whatever was in pockets, which wasn't much. In leaving the family business, I gave up any part of the business I might have had. And because of a tendency to spoil myself and have a bit too much fun, there wasn't much left for investing. The pressure was on, my wife was uncomfortable and sweating. However, I wasn't because I 'knew' I'd make it somehow / someway.

I might not be a billionaire like Gautam Adani and Ted Turner, but there is something the three of us have in common—at least, I like to think so. We grew up in an atmosphere that cultivated an entrepreneurial mind-set. We also had a desire to make more of ourselves by not accepting the status quo. We knew we had more to offer, be, do, and receive in our lives. We had a seed of creation, cultivation, and self-empowerment—an inner knowing that no matter what, we would find a way.

The three of us were raised in families that had their own businesses. No matter how big or small those businesses were, they were made up of the same basic elements. Entrepreneurship was in our DNA, but it was for us to follow that path. Just having that strand of DNA doesn't guarantee success. There are countless stories of siblings in similar situations where one made it and the other didn't.

If you don't have the seed of entrepreneurship in your DNA, don't fret. Just because you don't have this seed to water or cultivate from your family genetics or have had no influence from friends, parents, or teachers doesn't mean you can't make it. The entrepreneur mind-set, personality, character, and will are things that can be developed. You just have to want it enough.

"Entrepreneur" just denotes that you recognize that you're doing things across disciplines and that you're blazing your own path.

—Pharrell Williams

Entrepreneurs may not have traditional jobs or be on the time clock like conventional employees. They work un-clockable hours and are measured only by the level of success their companies attain, the wealth they personally accrue, and the wisdom and knowledge they gain by the trials, tribulations, failures, and rewards of such an endeavor.

I mentioned earlier that when you do what you love and get exhilarated and have a passion for it, it's not a job. An entrepreneur's job could be considered making sure that all ventures owned are functioning properly or developing new products / services or revolutionizing an entire industry or market place. There is plenty of work. It takes a lot of effort, will, and tenacity to get through it all, not to mention overcoming the resistance you'll meet from competitors, friends, family, and even your own mind.

Entrepreneurship is a road of learning. If a project, business, or idea fails, that doesn't mean you are a failure. Learn from mistakes, yours and others', and it's not failure—so long as you don't keep repeating it. The life of an entrepreneur is a roller-coaster ride of uncertainty for most of the journey, until true passive income is created in multiple avenues. In the beginning, you're never really certain if anything will succeed or where your money will come from month-to-month.

The relationship, mental, and emotional challenges met along the way are truly trying. However, there is an inner certainty that it will work out, some way and somehow. Building that inner muscle of certainty and being able to see the right direction takes time, practice, and patience. It is a way of life, dealing, seeing, and taking action—not a thing you just use once in a while.

You'll read some of what it takes to be an entrepreneur throughout the book. It has to be mentioned because it is the reason the Pitch, as we now know it, exists. Without the Entrepreneur, the Pitch wouldn't be so famous. I want this to be as much about Pitching as possible and show you that it's more than a performance. Since pitching is only associated with the entrepreneur's world nowadays,

I believe that in order to present a great pitch that gets attention, you must understand this world—or at least have a 'real' good clue about it.

The challenge is the initial jump from safety to entrepreneurship and understanding that success is yours to create, in business and life.

The Pitch and Verbal Marketing

Basically, you're selling a world as an actor, right? I mean it's like any sales person: if you believe in your product, you know your product, you sell it a lot better.

—*Paul Walker*

Chapter 1
What Is the Pitch?

You can't sell anything if you can't tell anything.

—Beth Comstock

The Pitch is derived from its original and traditional version, the Elevator Pitch. The Business Dictionary actually defines *elevator pitch* as "a very concise presentation of an idea covering all of its critical aspects, and delivered within a few seconds (the approximate duration of an elevator ride)."

That's it in a nutshell. Okay, book done. Now you know what a Pitch is—good luck and happy pitching. Of course, the power isn't in knowing what a pitch is, it's in knowing how to make a pitch what it's intended to be.

The pitch has taken on an entirely new persona and a life of its own since the old days of the elevator pitch. Now it's the king of the start-up world. It's become a key element in business development, fundraising, team-building and exposure for new entrepreneurs and start-up businesses. However, it seems to me that the pitch has not gotten the respect it deserves. Attention it has for sure, but respect it lacks. Since it is such a primary feature of the start-up world, I wonder why.

There are pitch competitions, business-development seminars, huge start-up events, government funded programs—you name it. There is everything and anything to give start-ups exposure, guidance, and funding from both competitions and interested investment angels. It's a subculture of the business world that is becoming a prime business culture, if it isn't already by the time I'm done writing this.

In addition, there are business incubators all over the place, especially in Europe and the Nordic and Scandinavian areas. They offer a ton of business training, mentorship, and think tanks. The pitch is front and center at all these conventions, one-day and two-day power start-up events, and regional conferences (Nordic, Scandinavian, Silicon Valley). You can't do anything in the start-up environment without it having to do with a pitch.

The pitch is so important that it ought to be given a lot more respect. Basically, without it, you don't get the exposure, funding, or team structure it can offer. It has the potential to take your idea, concept, product, or service to a whole new level quickly.

The Pitch isn't something only for the start-up world, as it's perceived to be. Remember, it started out as short form sales verbiage to gain a potential customer. The pitch, if devised properly, can be a useful tool your entire business life. The pitch is a Verbal Marketing tool and if done right can be very powerful. The Pitch's power is in drawing people in instead of pushing something onto them. The Pitch's power is in drawing people in instead of pushing something onto them.

WOM Marketing is a widely-used term used referring when someone talks about a product or service to their peers, publishes on social media... to promote what they like and it drives sales of that product or service up via their word mouth marketing.

Verbal Marketing is what I call and use to describe more directed and intended communication to promote a Product or service in conversation based on its many possible reflections of value. If marketing is a Method in which Advertising happens, then Verbal Marketing is the language design to deliver (advertise a product or service of its best value perspective).

Verbal Marketing is the skill of communicating Value in a way that **attracts** customers, funding angels, company interests... It is language by design to attract based on value representing benefits in the case of solving a problem, preventing one or enhancing something.

The pitch is the perfect networking tool—far more than in the old days of going to a cocktail party or networking event where you hand out business cards to a bunch of people who don't care, don't really need your services, and are (if you're lucky) just being polite. I'd take presenting to a room full of potentials and people who want to be there over having to talk to people all night in hope of finding that right connection. When you pitch, they find you.

The pitch is an event at which those who show up are interested and want to see your stuff. They are there for you, and you are front and center with all their attention. Yet so many don't take it seriously enough and avoid pitching like the plague. The pitch offers so much value, and yet so many don't use it to their advantage or with the right attitude or training and preparation.

The opportunities that the pitch positions you to have are incredible. We didn't have this when I started out—people waiting to see what you have and to hear your story, all while actually being interested, let alone people with money waiting for a great product or service like yours. Sure, there were always funding angels, but they weren't lining up to see you.

More commonly we had the banks, who weren't always interested or willing. Then there was always the last-ditch effort to turn up a lost rich uncle. Now, imagine this, me yelling this from a rooftop at you with a megaphone in hand: "You have people lining up to see what you have. They pay entrance fees for tickets to see what you offer, take it *serious* and Go and Pitch!"

Team members, customers, and especially funding angels are all there for the taking. All you have to do is show up and give the best presentation and most educated business model. Look at it this way: the worst that can happen is nobody likes your idea, and you look at it as market research. At least you have a public opinion and you can decide to restructure, redesign, or trash the whole thing altogether. No matter what, it pays to pitch.

The pitch is essential to the development of your start-up, so use it to your advantage; take it seriously and respect it. Keep reading and take advantage of the information about pitches, and you will better respect the pitch while learning what it takes to create one that demands respect.

Here are two different perspectives of personal experiences with a pitch. The first is from Lina, the owner of a start-up – Smooth it. Whom I had the pleasure to work with personally and see her development and growth, not only in pitching, but business and personal growth as well. And the second is from a woman that shared a story at a Start-Up event in Turku, Finland after seeking funding at a bank.

> It was a small conference room with men in suits from different countries and they were all staring at me. My heart was beating, my chest felt heavy, it was difficult to breathe and as I spoke my voice started crackling. The only thought I had was, "I could either open the door and run or continue the next 12 minutes and finish this – it's only twelve minutes". My first real presentation – the longest twelve minutes of my life.
>
> One year ago I started my company called Smooth it together with my workmate. In one year I have learned so much and the new experiences have made me much more confident.
>
> It was in Berlin and I was presenting our business in a global entrepreneur competition, competing to get a place to the upcoming finals in Bangkok. I like to *show up* and I am very competitive so I was pretty sure I could handle it and that it would go well.

One month before the competition I was excited and telling my mom about it. She was very excited too and was offering to me help if I needed. However, she asked me with a serious tone in her voice if I had really started to prepare for my presentation and had I determined properly the judging criteria. I answered quickly and a bit cocky," yes". But at the same time I answered I became aware that maybe I wasn't prepared at all. And that mom was right, but I didn't want to admit that.

Mom's suspicion about my preparation for the presentation gave me a lot of pressure, so I thought twice about my readiness. It was like a drop from the clouds back to earth. I could not believe that I thought I would just walk up there and present. I needed to practice! So after arguing with my mom, I started practicing. And I practiced every day until the wee hours.

And there I was, standing all tensed up in front of an audience, in the headquarter bank of Berlin, having my presentation with the feelings I mentioned earlier. And to my surprise, guess what, I got the place to the finals in Bangkok.

I was very happy and very grateful, especially to my mom who only thought of what's best for me and put the pressure on me to practice. After the presentation I understood how important the practicing was and that I needed to become better for the final round.

That's when I met Dean DiNardi, the author of this book and an amazing business developer and pitch trainer. DiNardi offered his time to help me with my next presentation for Bangkok. One big thing I have learned after meeting DiNardi and after starting my own business is that, take in all the help that is offered, learn to know your weaknesses and strengths and don't try to do everything by yourself. Because that is not how business works. As Steve Jobs once said; Great things in business are never done by one person. They're done by a team of people.

Even if I had practiced by myself and become a little bit better every time, I didn't recognize the fixable spots in my presentation. But DiNardi did, and after many cups of coffee and tea and time after time re-writing the presentation and practicing it in front of an audience, the fixable spots started to decrease. And the wee hours got closer until it was only one day left and I got this messages from Dean:

You kick ass girl - go get them in Bangkok.
Stay focused on the script... don't stray
with random banter (talk).
And for the most importantly - Breathe!
Relax in the knowing that you know
your company.
Good luck! Let me know how it goes...
safe returns.

Dean DiNardi

It gave me confidence. And there I stood again in front of the men in their suits, but this time I was smiling and waiting for the sign to let me start my presentation. And it started, I didn't feel any heartbeats, I did breathe and speak clear. I was present and connected to the audience. I felt good.

We didn't win the competition but all the learning, new contacts and experiences through the journey, made me already feel like a winner. The journey continues and there's plenty to learn more. When I became an entrepreneur I thought it was obvious that when you start a business you can automatically present or represent it too. But it's not. And there will come many unexpected moments when you need to stand up and present or pitch. I learned that always prepare well and anticipate, be humble and not cocky thinking too highly of yourself. Still believe in yourself and your business, work hard, ask for help, fail and try again, and step by step the success will be yours. Myself, I'm still taking the baby steps but imagining the big ones.

-Lina-

Lina now is opening a second Smooth-it stand. And as we talk, I see how much growth she has undergone in just one year. She had fostered the mindset of an entrepreneur and it show. The work on the pitch development we did together helped her to identify with her company and its purpose more clearly. In turn it gave a higher level of confidence, especially after owning her space in front of those suits and representing it.

Secondly, soon after I met Lina, I met a young lady at a start-up event who told me a story of a time when she first started out and went for funding at a bank:

> I had just got done telling the loan agent about my business plan and the reason for wanting to have this business, and she got up, excused herself, and left the room. She neglected to tell me where she was heading or when she would be returning. I assumed she would be back shortly.
>
> After several minutes, I saw her returning from down the hall. She was accompanied by a sharply dressed businessman in his mid-fifties, it seemed. I started to sweat out of uncertainty over what was about to happen—although I relaxed at the fact he was not a security guard. It's amazing the things that run through your mind when you're nervous.
>
> The two of them entered the room, and then the loan agent introduced the

man as the bank loan manager. After
introductions, the manager asked if I
could tell him my story and my purpose
for the loan. Surprised and uncertain of
where this was going, I did so.

After I had finished the same story
I had told the loan agent, the manager
reached out his hand and congratulated
me on obtaining the loan.

He went on to say that he had never
met anyone with such conviction and
motivation coming for a loan. He went on
to mention that the agent had gone to him
because she wasn't able to clearly make
a decision for my loan. I got it because of
my determination and solid plan.

After the young lady finished her story, she confided
in me that afterward the agent had told her that she
didn't have suitable loan creditability or securities—
simply not enough load history or requirements to
secure the loan. But her conviction inspired the
agent to ask higher authorities. The bank manager
further mentioned that he believed there was no way
for failure, with either the business or holding up her
end of the loan obligation.

The manager told her that her energy reminded
him of a racehorse that was destined to win being

held back at the gate, just waiting for it to open. In addition to getting the loan, she succeeded in paying it back earlier then its maturity date.

Now, for sure, this doesn't happen to everyone, yet it was a pitch. The elements that got her the loan are the same elements that need to be in a pitch. I wrote this book with the intention of offering a different perspective on the pitch. I hope to present you with reasons to respect it and learn how to use it to your advantage in getting what you want.

I have thirty-ish years combined experience as a business developer, personal life strategist and theatrical trained professional. I have worked in both the traditional business world and the entrepreneur's world, working for others as well as owning my own companies. In addition, to polish this off, I am a professionally trained and practiced actor, director, producer, and writer for film and theater. As well have assisted start-up's, individuals and business professionals to succeed in their endeavors through my personal life strategies and personally developed system for success and the mindset.

Through the combined elements of my experience, I have the perfect skill set to assist you in developing your pitch and offer business development strategies. Along with developing the mindset to support it all and drive the train of success all the way to the station and any other destination it wished to travel throughout your life.

The pitch can be so powerful in getting you the funding you're looking for, team members who will line up at your door to work with you, and customers with an overload of orders waiting to ring in—but you have to embrace it. Embracing the pitch is like eating a can of spinach for Popeye. For those who don't know who Popeye is, he's an American cartoon character who, after eating a can of spinach, grows muscles and always beats the bad guys. I hope this book is like a can of spinach for you to grow your pitch, presentation and entrepreneur muscles.

Brainchild

Chapter 2
Vision

In the Bible, there is a phrase that illustrates the idea of creation—the actual and simple idea of what it takes to create something. The entry goes something like this: "And God said, let there be light, and there was light ..." It is thought that starts the train of creation rolling into actual being-ness. You don't have to be God and ask for there to be light. Stand for a moment and announce out load, "I am strong, I am confident, I am willing." What did you feel? It started something in you, a feeling, a shift. Thought is the seed of creation and emotion (the *why*) is the water that feeds it.

Consider anything that you have done today. Before you did it, you had to think it. Even if you didn't think it that very moment and it was second nature—brushing your teeth, combing your hair, going to the bathroom. You had to have the thought initially at some point before it became a trained habit. First there is thought, then emotion stirred by the notion, and then a demand for action. That action (or decision not to act) is based on your level of fear, need, and courage, as well as the value you put on it. That action is the doing that is (or isn't) manifesting the original thought into existence.

One of the first elements of success or achieving a goal is having vision. Vision is seeing what's not there yet. It's putting energy, attention, and focus on where you want to go and what you want to have happen. You can do this with your pitches.

When you know you are going to pitch, in the several days leading up to it, envision the performance. Visualize and have thoughts of positive action. A setback comes when people are unsure or afraid of saying where they want to go or uncertain in the belief that it's even possible. Sometimes making a decision feels like a lot of pressure. What if I look like a fool? What if I say the wrong thing? The same thing tends to happen with our visions and ambitions. What if pursuing that vision is a waste of time? What if I reach it and am disappointed because it's not what I expected?

> *If you limit your choices only to what seems possible or reasonable, you disconnect yourself from what you truly want, and all that is left is a compromise.*
>
> —*Robert Frizt*

How many times have you felt frustrated because you followed what you thought would be the best choice based on love, on advice from others, or because it was the expected thing to do (based on religion, politics, social circles, and the like)? Without a clear vision of what you want, you'll always find yourself lost, confused, aimless, and doing things because of others. Make sure your vision is *your* vision and not something created from the fragments of outside influences.

When you pitch, you need to demonstrate certainty about your product, service, team, ability to deliver, and of course, yourself. This means you must believe in your brainchild and give it time while putting the time in. Keep in mind your big vision and always feel inspired by it.

Another limitation comes when you want to go everywhere all at once. You want to support your loved ones financially, but you also want to take a chance on a new idea or business that might be financially risky at first but makes you feel alive. You want to know you'll have the time and money to take that trip around the world that's been years in the planning.

If you want to have your cake and eat it too, at least make sure the cake is made of the ingredients you want, not somebody else's recipe. Doing this takes time, which takes away the common idea of having your cake and eating it too—the now factor. Believe me, I tried several times to have my cake and eat it too. I was never really satisfied. It wasn't until I gave up the cake that I understood this. Then I started to mix the ingredients for the cake *I wanted to eat,* not the one that just happened to be there.

There are times when you might travel a bit and forget where you are going or become lost or sidetracked, meandering up and down streets or passing exits. I've done that one. You've forgotten your original destination, and more importantly, your original vision. More common is the road trip of distraction—when you are heading toward your destination and then find yourself doing other things, thinking about other stuff, and unintentionally heading in a different direction. These distractions are bad accidents on the road to winning and creating your dreams, goals, and aspirations, especially if they happen often.

Incidentally, bad habits are usually based on fear. You haven't built the strength in your automatic muscle group. You need to build muscles of consistency for actions and behaviors that support the direction you want. You need to build success-orientated response muscles. This is a place where self-evaluation comes in handy. Know where you really are in order to build the muscles needed to take you where you really want to go.

Many times, we assume the solution is "work harder." Action is definitely part of achieving a vision, but driving faster in the wrong direction is not the way to achieve anything. Stay focused on your vision and see it as possible. If you see it as possible, then when you pitch, others will be more likely see it possible, and you'll get the support you need.

Vision is having a destination. In order to reach that destination, you must have a clear road map. A pitch is also like a road map. You can reach your destination more efficiently, easily, and quickly if you have a good one. When you pitch, you illustrate that you know where you are going and you know the vision and purpose behind your idea, concept, service, or product.

Look at the pitch as not just a performance but also an outline or tool that helps you stay focused and on the road to your destination. You will more easily be able to develop your vision for your product or service and what it is, how it does what it does, why you thought of it, and who it's for. Although this will lead to success, remember it's a process and doesn't guarantee success at that exact point in time. There can be a number of detours, accidents, and hazards along the road ahead. But you are an entrepreneur and that means you'll find a way, even if it's a different one. It's fulfilling your ultimate vision that counts – financial security, a new house, cars, college for your children, personal capability (knowing it was possible, self-confidence)....

So how does someone look to develop a clear vision? First, decide whether you're looking at your personal or business vision. You'll need both. For a business vision, you can use the pitch-deck in the back of the book as a short-form business plan to help you sum up and focus on what's important. For a personal vision, decide what you want in your life, how you want it to look, and the quality of life you seek. It's your life; decide what you want and how you want it to be. Create a vision statement for both your business and personal vision. There is plenty of information out there on how to develop vision statements. For instance, Stephen Covey has a ton of books and programs that are valuable.

After determining which vision you are creating, spend some quality time with the idea. Instead of latching onto the first "sounds good" that comes to mind, ask, *What do I really want from this? Where do I want it to go? What do I want for myself personally from the experience and from a business in general?* Get started with the general questions of what, why, how, and who.

Some people are able to picture their vision best when spending quiet time by themselves at the beach or taking a walk in nature. Others feel it in the hustle and bustle of busy streets—New York City, London, Helsinki. Others like to write their thoughts in a journal and ruminate on them a bit before creating a vision statement. I have found it useful to put together a think tank with peers, educators, or business specialists. It's a great way to get insight not otherwise thought of.

Bill Gates, Steve Jobs, Henry Ford, Rev. Jesse Jackson—all had a vision and had to work for it. Their vision didn't manifest overnight, and it didn't come easily. When you do the work, it's more likely that the universe will reflect your efforts back when the time is right. My point is that there is no luck, only effort made for a vision that eventually says, "I'm ready."

Vision is believing in something that is much bigger than you can imagine at the immediate time of thinking it. No matter how silly and outside of current technological, emotional, mental, and physical standards it might seem at the time, you forge forward with a belief in its development. It's personal. Sometimes the pursuit is believing in something that nobody else believes in. From my perspective, that's vision. When you pitch your business idea, you are giving your audience a taste of that vision and making them hungry for more— for that second meeting that offers more time to indulge on the morsels left out of the pitch.

I can't tell you how many pitches I have seen where presenters showed little to no enthusiasm for this *thing* that they had worked so hard to develop and put so much time into. I sometimes feel as if pitchers present like they are talking about their sleeping dog or a blank sheet of paper—which, incidentally, I think a blank sheet of paper has more potential than they do when they pitch. You have to make yourself and what you're presenting jump off the blank page, at least a little. Color and the life of a story makes the blank page more interesting and draws people in.

Your vision in the pitch is when you tell about the product or service and imagine future development, angles, products, or opportunities that could come from it. When you see this clearly and are excited and motivated by it, your audience will see that and feel the same.

We are limited not by our abilities, but by our vision.

—Unknown

Goals

Our goals can only be reached through a vehicle of a plan, in which we must fervently believe, and upon which we must vigorously act. There is no other route to success.

—Pablo Picasso

Chapter 3
Mapping

*Setting goals is the first step in turning
the invisible into the visible.*
—*Tony Robbins*

It seems that no one really knows where the term
sales pitch originated. The only evidence I was able
to find established the pitch around the late 1940s,
with no real connection or definition. I think that
the pitch simply evolved through association with a
sign of the times. When American baseball and the
stereotypical modern style of a salesperson were at
their height, the baseball pitch became a metaphor
for the sales pitch to springboard from. The sales
pitch is the need to deliver important information
in a fast, effective, and direct way—just like a ball
speeding toward home plate.

What inspires you about your vision? If you've
taken it further than just a vision and actually started
to develop things, what has been your motivation to

do so? The answers to questions like these are what keep you on your goal path. Vision is necessary, but it's the hidden motivations behind it that propel the vision forward. In order to give a necessary forward thrust, you must have a strong enough reason *why*. If you don't have a strong why, you won't put time into creating and actually working on or completing your goals. And then there is no reason for goals.

Just like the baseball player with the goal of getting the ball to home plate as fast and unhittable as possible or the sales man finding ways to make his customer desire his product / service. It's their why that's the driving force behind their actions.

Without a strong why, goals are empty promises, simply because the fuel won't be available to either start or finish them. Goals without a driving force will get you nowhere other than where you already are. With that said, much of goal-setting is knowing why you want to get somewhere or do something.

When you pitch, one important element is why you are doing the thing you're pitching—the story that drives your purpose. More often than not, it is your story that people are drawn to, and this opens doors—especially if a funding angel is on the fence or sees that your idea needs some extra attention. This individual has to determine whether it's worth it for him or her to put the extra effort (time and money) into it. Often it's the personal story, the power of the why, that persuades such funders to go for it and take the chance on you. Your personality is also a factor, but we'll get to that later.

There are two types of goals to look at. The first are your personal goals. What do you want and why? Where do you want to go and why? Remember, it's not just about the what and where—the why is the power source. The why will carry you through adversity and tough times. It will be the thing that ultimately keeps life in your vision.

The second goal is your business and actual product or service. It's traditional to have a one-, three-, five-, and ten-year plan. This is important because you need benchmarks and a clear depiction of where you need to go in order to accomplish a goal or task.

Ask yourself if you are satisfied with where you are in your financial affairs, health, relationships, and career. What have you set as your benchmarks for success in each of those areas? What goals have you set for yourself personally or in your career or business life?

As the saying goes, "Life is what happens while you're busy making plans." If those plans are important to you and have your life's values in them, they won't get left out or missed. In order to create that kind of goal, you must know what you want. However, there is a flip side to this: Consider also what you don't want. Most people forget to do this, but it is just as, if not more, important to have an idea of what you don't want as it is knowing what you do want. The trick is to focus on what you want, knowing that you can raise a red flag if the *don'ts* start popping up in your life or business.

Where your mind goes, energy flows.
—*Ernest Holmes*

Have you ever known people who always complain or mention what doesn't happen, can't happen, is not happening for them? For every ten time they mention not having something, they only mention once what they would like or what they can have. They are too focused on what they don't want or how bad things are all the time to recognize what they want and how things can be. This is also contributed to that mindset we spoke about earlier.

As important as it is to know what you don't want, don't get stuck there. Focus on what you do want and be open to finding ways to achieve it. If you're in the *can't* rut, it is not always easy to get out, but it is possible. Start with baby steps. As long as you have the will, you will find a way and remember your why. It can be as small as waking up in the morning and making it to the bathroom to brush your teeth because you don't want them to rot.

In a pitch, you need an "it will happen" attitude. It helps to focus on a tighter plan and only narrow in on what to do to get it done. The more focused you are on what you want and how you are going to achieve it, the easier it is to articulate (speak) it. In my experience, that is a common problem with pitchers: articulating their ideas. Keeping it short and concise. Know exactly what you want to say. Can you describe your idea, product, or service in six to ten words?

When looking to structure goals for personal or business needs, it's a good idea to start with the small and then get bigger. This is different than when you envision your goals, dreams.... Then you start big and narrow in. For example, to use the funnel model, instead of funneling things in, you are funneling things out. J. C. Penney was a man who didn't mince words. He once said, "Give me a stock clerk with a goal, and I'll give you a man who will make history. Give me a man with no goals, and I'll give you a stock clerk." You want to set goals so you have purpose and direction in your actions.

Not to stress you out, but if you don't have goals, you may find yourself waking up one night in a cold sweat, realizing you've lived an aimless life. Welcome to the midlife crisis—or worse yet, the point of being too old to do anything about it, the point where your dreams and aspiration truly break off from any possibility of happening. Yes, I am trying to spook you! I hope it's working.

Goal-setting is a powerful process for thinking about your ideal future and motivating yourself to turn your vision of this future into reality. The process of setting goals helps you choose where you want to go in life and in your business. The great thing about goal-setting is that you can do it anytime. Set, change, adapt ... whatever it takes to get the end result met. Your goals should be evaluated frequently. Make them clear to follow and understand. However, don't get stuck in constantly changing and adapting them, or you will never actually succeed at accomplishing them.

It might sound like it takes some time and effort to develop, identify, and implement your vision and goals. It does, but if it means that much to you and you have a strong why, do it. Your dreams and passions are worth your efforts.

The unexamined life isn't worth living.
— Socrates

A little food for thought: examining your life to find out where you are, where you want to go, and how quickly and most productively you can get there has so much value. A common goal-setting technique most of you might have heard is the acronym SMART. Those initials stand for *specific, measurable, attainable, realistic,* and *timely.*

S = Specific

You want your goals to be specific. This means the goal is clear and unmistakable, without fancies, impulses, or clichés. Definitely no maybes, could bes, or might bes. For goals to be specific, they must express exactly what's expected, why it's important, who's involved, where it's going to happen, and which attributes are important. A specific goal will usually answer the five *W* questions:

- *What* do I want to accomplish?
- *Why* do I want to accomplish this goal?
- *Who* is involved?
- *Where* will it happen?
- *Which* requirements and constraints are involved?

When a goal is specific, you'll know when you've achieved it. Setting goals is like connecting the dots on a map to get you from A to B to C to D. It's an efficient means to an end.

This is definitely an attribute of a pitch-deck. When you present, you need to know these questions and answers. It's the basics of your plan. Also, be specific. Most contest pitches are three minutes long, and you need to choose the right information to fill the time. Many pitches fall short on information in fear of going over time, and others put way too much information in and end up going way over. It takes time and skill to construct a pitch.

M = Measurable

The second principle stresses the need for concrete criteria for measuring progress toward the attainment of a goal. The thought behind this is that if a goal is not measurable, it is not possible to know whether you or a team is making progress toward successful completion. Measuring progress is supposed to help you and your team stay on track and reach target dates. This offers you the experience and exhilaration of achievement that spurs everyone on for continued efforts that are required to reach the ultimate goal or vision.

For proper measurement, indicators should be quantifiable. A measurable goal will usually answer questions like how much? how many? how will I know when it is accomplished—what will it look like? Using the road map analogy, the steps in this process are turns in the road on the way to your destination. They can be measured. This will help you stay on track and give you reason to celebrate when you accomplish the goal. And you should celebrate! And isn't this exactly what is needed in developing a pitch? What you're doing and how your're getting there.

A = Attainable

Are your goals achievable and realistic? An attainable goal may stretch you or your team, but it is not so extreme as to be impossible. Goals should be neither out of reach nor below standard performance.

When you identify goals that are most important, you begin to figure out ways you can make them come true. You develop the attitudes, abilities, skills, creativity, and financial capacity to reach them (often from unfamiliar and unexpected places). The theory states that an attainable goal may cause goal-setters to identify previously overlooked opportunities to bring themselves closer to the achievement of their goals.

An achievable goal will usually answer the question, "How can the goal be accomplished?" and "How realistic is the goal based on other constraints?" Baking twenty-four dozen donuts in ten minutes is not an attainable goal. Acquiring five hundred new customers in one week, with no skills, connections, or marketing ability is not an attainable goal. I think this one speaks for itself in every format. In a pitch, if you don't know your information, you probably won't attain funding.

R = Relevant

The fourth measure stresses the importance of choosing goals that matter. A bank manager's goal to make fifty peanut butter and jelly sandwiches by three o'clock in the afternoon may be specific, measurable, attainable, and time-bound, but it lacks relevance. Many times you will need support to accomplish a goal: resources, a champion voice, someone to knock down obstacles and see through the fog of impractical notions. Goals that are relevant will receive the needed support.

Relevant goals, when met, drive you, your team, and your organization forward. A goal that supports or is in alignment with other goals would be considered a relevant goal. With a relevant goal, you can answer yes to the following questions:

- Does this seem worthwhile?
- Is this the right time?
- Does this match our other efforts/needs?
- Am I the right person?
- Is it applicable in the current socioeconomic environment?

Every bit of information has to be relevant when you pitch. That means content and context must match, and the goals that you set have relevance for obtaining the ultimate goal. If you don't represent this in your pitch, your pitch will represent that you are too scattered and dreamy.

T = Timely

You don't want to meander toward your goal, but instead create grounded goals within a time frame, giving you and them a target date. Having a vague date sometime in the future will not cut it. Don't set *on* or *about* dates; you want to anchor your goal within a specific time frame. This will assure you or your team achieve the goal with higher probability on or before the target date.

Also, having specific dates and timetables puts pressure on you and/or your team to get them done. As you near the end of the timeline, you will be able to gauge the distance till the due date. If you're behind, you will feel the need and pressure to be more motivated. Timelines demand action.

This aspect of SMART keeps goals from being taken over by day-to-day happenings or crises. Time-bound goals will usually have answers to the following questions:

- When?
- What can I do six months from now?
- What can I do six weeks from now?
- What can I do today?

If it's realistic and has happened before, it can happen again.

If you present loose, "maybe," or "we think around ..." times, you convey uncertainty and a lack of commitment. You don't want investment angels to see this. This attitude will also push customers away because they want to know when *exactly* they can get something, not *maybe* or *around*. That's like getting them excited and then pulling the carpet out from under them. I think it's always better and safer to say a time far enough in the future that you can be sure of, rather than something sooner you may not be able to follow through on or that will appear to be an unattainable goal.

Desire is the key to motivation, but
it's determination and commitment to
an unrelenting pursuit of your goal, a
commitment to excellence, that will enable
you to attain the success you seek.
—Mario Andretti

Each SMART attribute is exactly what a pitch is made of. Take a look at the pitch-deck in the back of the book or any other one, for that matter. It has to have these qualities and attributes. A pitch has to be SMART.

Willingness

*Most people don't have that willingness
to break bad habits. They have a lot of
excuses and they talk like victims.*

—Carlos Santana

Chapter 4
What's It Worth?

> *We must be willing to get rid of the life*
> *we've planned so as to have the life that*
> *is waiting for us.*
> —*Joseph Campbell*

Willingness. It seems like a harmless word, but when you start to ask how willing you are to grow, to change, to forgive, to get what you want in life—well, it takes on a whole new meaning with a lot of value. However, let's keep it elementary for a moment.

We started this off with the notion of a brainchild—your vision, idea, concept, the thing you value and want to bring to the world. Now I ask you—what are you willing to do or become to see this happen? When we strive to achieve things in life, it is inevitable that we will be challenged to grow and change.

You will be faced with adversity, doubt, and financial and relationship challenges, to name a few. What will you do? Are you willing to fight for your idea, overcome fear, rethink uncertainty, or overcome financial or possible educational shortcomings? You don't need the answers now or before you begin, yet you do need the willingness to take a chance. This is also where having a strong why and success mindset comes in handy. The *why* motivates the *will* and the mindset support.

Are you willing to grow and change into the person you need to be in order to meet your goals, dreams, and aspirations of success? Of course you are, or you would not be here right now. However, what does this all mean? Does it really take so much?

Willingness varies from person to person based on tolerance and personal challenges in life. However, to not be willing is to be in resistance. How can you tell when you're in resistance? Resistance can show up in many ways. For starters, it's being unwilling to pitch because you are the tech guy or have the sniffles, especially if it's your brainchild on the line. Resistance is knowing what you should do but not doing it, or a nagging feeling that you need to take action that could lead to your greater good yet for most likely a self-convincing reason you don't take that action.

Resistance can also be subtler. Perhaps days, weeks, and months squeak by and you realize you've slowly been sinking in a certain area. Relationships are always on edge, financial matters ebb into the red, your health declines. You realize that the things that used to be great are now only good or fair to middling.

Mark Twain wrote that "courage is resistance to fear, mastery of fear, not absence of fear." This quote is perfect in the way that it says exactly what resistance is and how to overcome it. It's also very relevant to pitching. We'll mention that in a moment.

Resistance comes up in new challenges or situations that require unfamiliar actions. You back away, avoiding the uncertain road. You constantly wonder whether you've hesitated so long that the opportunity has passed or eked away. In my personal life, I've realized that willingness and resistance go hand and hand. There's a popular saying many of you might be familiar with: "What you resist, persist." At some point I had to ask, *Am I willing? Why am I not willing to approach what's been nagging and persisting in my life?*

I have been an entrepreneur my whole life. I was a part of a family business that was started by my grandfather from the ground up—the old-fashioned way—and passed to his children. It wasn't mine in the sense that I didn't build it. We helped expand it, but it wasn't the same for me. I wanted to build my own business, but I realized after years of thinking about it and trying to get out on my own why I wasn't succeeding at doing so.

First, I realized that *try* is not an action word. I had to be willing to step out even when there was just as much of a possibility of failure as success. I was afraid, and things were comfy where I was, but it wasn't what I wanted. I needed a strong reason to walk out into the unknown.

I needed to overcome my fears and inhibitions. I ultimately found the will to drive home the action of doing. It wasn't until I decided to accept that I was afraid that I was able to embrace it and let it go. Finding my will through a strong why helped me to accept my fear and find ways to work around it, eventually overcoming it.

As I mentioned earlier, I had the entrepreneurial seed within, but it was up to me to water it. The seed wouldn't grow on its own. I had to till the earth for new soil (acknowledging old ways, habits, and behaviors that didn't work toward my goals) and provide fertilizer (creating new behaviors and habits that did work) and water (action to see goals fulfilled). This is a good example of a success mindset. The thinking of finding the ways no matter what.

What does it look like to be willing? It's an ease, a calmness, and a sense of relaxing into a better way. It's dropping the shoulds and the can'ts and the what-ifs and instead taking a moment to be with the *what is* and the *what can be.* Build on small achievements, personal or otherwise.

Taking a breath—literally—and noticing the very present moment stops the roller coaster of thoughts that take us away from our present moment and experience. It also helps us put fear and apprehension into perspective. If you really want to see how this works, take a moment and repeat out loud, "I am willing." Take a breath and notice the feelings and thoughts that come up.

In her book *Fearless Living*, Rhonda Britton puts it simply by saying, "Being willing makes you able." When you drop the resistance, stories, and excuses, you find yourself lighter and more willing—more able—to allow and do. Just relax and receive. Feel how nice that is, and how freeing and empowering.

When you pitch, your willingness shines through your fear. The more you relax and accept fear instead of trying to hide it, the easier it is to put it backstage where it can't interfere with your pitch. Fear can be there without it controlling you.

I have looked at and worked with fear in my own life. I have found that looking at fear through being scared takes a lot of pressure off. I have found that fear tends to immobilize, while being scared leaves possibility. Try it. Instead of telling yourself you are afraid, simply say you're scared but you can work through it. Being scared is easier to accept and work through, while fear cripples.

One thing I have found important and powerful is to ask myself why or for what reason I am doing this. If your answer is not strong or you don't have a deeply important reason to pursue your goal till the end, you won't be willing to do whatever it takes. Willingness is more than a drive, an attitude, or a motivation that propels you forward. It is influenced by the depth of your perception and ability to see beyond your normal scope at the time. Being open and willing gives way to imagination and being able to envision—finding ways, people, funding, and whatever else is needed.

One thing I have learned is that if you want to succeed in business, you have to be willing to grow personally, and you will be challenged to do so. However, if you want to succeed in life, your personal character shouldn't clash with what you do for business. Eventually you will be forced to adjust your goals to match your values if you want to be happy, truly peaceful, successful, and not in resistance.

If you're reading these words, chances are you are hoping to evolve and not stay the same. You want to continue to grow as a person and experience all life has to offer. Even if that's pushing a little, it's a good reason to drop the resistance and become more willing. How would you like things to become easier in life or simply have what you really want? It can happen, if you are willing. Just dig inside of yourself and find your reason for taking action, your why.

When you support your pitch with a genuine why and a personal reason, people are attracted and value that. Pitch with Presence, Pizzazz, and Professionalism—that's my motto. When you deliver a pitch with the willingness to succeed, it's a whole different performance than one without. Just think of a movie and imagine an actor not willing to do what it takes to bring that character and story to life. The result would be boring, dull, and uninteresting. It would lose your attention and interest.

There comes a point when resistance is dropped and willingness is there. So what's next? It's time to move into action. The problem most people have is that they get into their heads and start a need-to litany, as in, "I need to do this and I need to do that and I need to do this, this, and this." Although you do need to take action, you don't want to end up in a place of analysis and paralysis.

If you get stuck in the endless loop of need tos, with the eternal list of items growing, that's the only action you'll take. The actionless action of thinking about and organizing all the things to do instead of actually doing anything. Instead, start with small steps, even baby steps, while remaining alert and aware of what comes next. A good place to start is challenging yourself to do little things that frighten you or are intimidating. Ask somebody on a date, eat something that wigs you out, take a trip alone. What are you willing to do to strengthen your courage, confidence, and will?

Previously, I advised you to celebrate. Do it whenever you achieve a goal. Little successes along the way amount to a ton of support, confidence-building, and encouragement during tough times and adversity. Do a football slam, fist pump—whatever it takes. Celebrate your achievements and willingness, especially when you have stretched outside your comfort zone to meet a goal. And it's ok to hide in the corner and do it, but eventually you'll stand in the middle of a crowd and shout, 'I did it'.

There is only one thing required to change your life, and that is willingness. You can do this. It's just a matter of getting out of your own way.

Perfectionism

Striving for excellence motivates you;
striving for perfection is demoralizing.

—Harriet Braiker

Chapter 5
Overcoming Perfectionism

But I am learning that perfection isn't what matters. In fact, it's the very thing that can destroy you if you let it.

—*Emily Giffin*

So many people don't do things that are important to them, including pitching, because they get stuck on how imperfectly they believe they will do it, even if they have never tried. Many think they are not perfect or good enough in public speaking, or they have to be something more special than what they are or might be. But they don't. You don't!

Many people throw around the idea of being a perfectionist with a great deal of pride, but living life as a perfectionist can be a nightmare. The idea of never being satisfied with *good enough* means condemning yourself to always striving for better, better, better, and not enjoying the blessings life has for you right now or that is in the process of growing.

One solution is to work harder and strive or push for better – steps of improvement; that's growing and not settling. However, insisting on perfection is crippling and demoralizing. Your pitch is not going to be perfect the first or possibly the tenth time. Ironically, when you think you've done a bad job, others will inevitably think you did great. That's why you need to just get out there and do it.

I have learned that you will never exceed your own expectations. It's good to have goals and high values to hold yourself to or want as a standard in your life—or even for others to uphold. But to hold yourself or others to any standard of perfectionism is unfair, unappreciative, demoralizing, and crippling ... in addition to being a disaster waiting to happen and definitely not the road to success.

Have goals, work for them, and expect to meet them. Pursue your goals instead of false ideals of perfection. Perfection is a false ideal because things are always perfect the way they are in the true grand scheme of life. Perfection doesn't really exist; it can't be achieved. There are endless possibilities of how things or people can be. It's a little thing called evolution. Life is only imperfect in our limited perception of ourselves or others.

A very common self-sabotaging and goal-crippling pattern in the obsession with perfection—and one that is often unseen, as it is tightly woven through the actions of one's daily choices—is to become so obsessed and worried about making things perfect that you never even begin the journey. It becomes an excuse for never getting started.

Dr. David Burns, an adjunct professor in the Department of Psychiatry and Behavioral Sciences at the Stanford University School of Medicine, puts it this way: "Aim for success, not perfection. Never give up your right to be wrong, because then you will lose the ability to learn new things and move forward with your life. Remember that fear always lurks behind perfectionism. Confronting your fears and allowing yourself the right to be human can, paradoxically, make yourself a happier and more productive person."

We talked about confronting, not ignoring, your fears earlier in the context of willingness. Here, in the context of overcoming perfectionism, we would say something like: Be willing to do it but go easy on yourself, for you're not perfect and only learn by your mistakes. Willingness seeks to reach beyond fear.

There's a lot to be said for mistakes. They are valuable in that they demonstrate to you what not to do and what doesn't work. Most of us have heard how many times Thomas Edison tried to invent the lightbulb, and how he failed miserably time after time. In fact, when it finally continued to burn, he just expected it to fail and waited for it to go out. And waited. And waited. Can you imagine the feeling of exhilaration that started to grow when he realized that it wasn't going to flicker out this time—that he had done it? It must have been amazing! But it would never have happened if he didn't stick with it. Willingness meets imperfection with a plan for a goal through an ultimate vision.

If you suffer from perfectionism, keep the following general ideas in mind to overcome a tendency that could be keeping you from success.

1. **Take it easy on yourself.** No one succeeds with a drill sergeant screaming in his or her ear all the time. It's also not a matter of one giant leap from idea to success but rather a series of steps along the way (that you celebrate). Practice, practice, practice—one pitch after another. Practice and enjoy the journey. Isn't there a saying about it being the journey, not the destination? It's really both, isn't it?

   Also, be willing to release your idea of what has to be perfect, especially you. A good way to apply this to pitching is to take part in a lot of little pitch sessions, including contests (preferably those where you don't much care if you win or lose). Practice in front of a mirror and record your pitch. It won't be perfect and that's okay; however, having the right elements is important and necessary. This, by the way, doesn't excuse you from practicing or not knowing your pitch. After all, isn't that the work?

Practice, practice, practice. Know your business. Most importantly, enjoy it and have fun. Play with it.

2. **Take it easy on others.** Forcing your ideas of what's perfect on others is a sure road to tense relationships and extreme stress. People don't like to feel controlled or manipulated or bullied. They definitely don't like their perceived weaknesses called out. Consider things from others' perspective and do unto others as you would like them to do unto you.

When you pitch, understand that you might not wow everyone there, or anyone at all, and that it might not be you. Don't be mad or upset at people if they don't like your product, service, or company. The idea just isn't ideal for them. Don't give up based on others' reactions, ideas, and principles. Don't push your perceptions, values, or needs on them. Instead, value the fact that there is another view or way. Use it to evaluate, and say thank you.

3. **See the funny side of life.** The tension felt by a strong sense of perfectionism means there's little room for seeing the humor in

life. And life is funny! When you look around and relax your standards, you'll see a lot of opportunity to laugh, which feels good. It will also help you out when things don't go exactly according to plan. Laugh at yourself. If you make a mistake or something appropriate and relevant pops up during a pitch, share it. If the crowd feels relaxed as you do, they will be more receptive. Laughter makes people more relaxed. Warning – don't force humor in your pitch; that does not work.

I recommend a book called *The Gifts of Imperfection* in which Brené Brown, PhD, a leading expert on shame, authenticity, and belonging, shares what she's learned from a decade of research on the power of wholehearted living—a way of engaging with the world from a place of worthiness.

You'll very rarely if ever hit the mark perfectly the first time. A child who tumbles after trying out his first steps doesn't stay on the floor forever thinking, "That's it. I guess I wasn't meant to walk." Instead, he gets up and tries again, all the while not seeking to be perfect but simply to do.

Relationships

*I just enjoy being onstage and relating
to the audience.*

—Idina Menzel

Chapter 6
It's All About Relationships

*Entrepreneurs may be brutally honest,
but fostering relationships with partners
and building enduring communities
requires empathy, self-sacrifice, and
a willingness to help others without
expecting anything in return.*

—Ben Parr

Relationships are important in so many ways, in pitching as well as everything else. The better your relationship is with your company (or product or service), the better you can convey it to people. That actually is the heart of the pitch. Isn't that simply what a pitch is—relaying your business, idea, or service to others? The key words are relay and relate—relationship.

Whether it's a one-, three-, or twelve-minute pitch, the trick is always finding the best way to relate the information. The only way to do that is to have the best relationship with what you're talking about. When you present onstage or in any other forum, in front of people, you are transparent. If you're not feeling it, they will see that; but more than that, they won't feel it either. Your thoughts, emotions, and most definitely attitude are visible to the audience even if you think you are hiding them.

The flip side of this is that if you are authentically hiding your stuff; I mean, if you are aware and not trying to pretend or be untruthful about anything, you can hide a bit of what might be going on in your personal life in order to get through the performance. In this way, the authenticity will outweigh and help the hiding. It's when you think you're fooling the audience that you really care when you don't that you are transparent in a bad way.

Start with your relationship with yourself. When you present and aren't being authentic or real, others sense that. When you are fearful, uncertain, confused, unrehearsed, trying too hard to impress, and hiding false cares, people notice! But don't fret. They also notice when you are confident, prepared, certain about what you're presenting and really invested. We get that you might not appear to care that day (maybe you're having a bad hair day), but you do care authentically about it.

When you start a business of any kind, you have to write a business plan. In its simplest form, you will write what you are doing, why, and how—even if it's a five-sentence form for small (very small) personal business, like selling lemonade. If you don't physically write it, this is the process you think of in your mind. With larger-scale businesses, you will need to write out a formal business plan, especially when applying for funding. This business plan is long and full of details that mostly do not need to be represented in your pitch. But you need to know the information in your business plan to be able to pitch. You need the idea, marketing, competition, and financials to present in a pitch.

Have you ever taken a close look or even a distant look at a pitch-deck? Take a look at the one at the end of this book. What do you see? You should see a basic business-plan outline. A pitch-deck is a way to have an easy and clear relationship with your business, product, or service. A relationship is a connection, and when we have a connection, we relate better. When we relate better, we communicate and understand more clearly. We also are more open and receptive to things.

The better your relationship with your business is, the better your pitch will be. Even if you're not great at delivering the pitch, the information will be great, and that counts for a lot, especially if you are being authentic.

There is another type of business relationship not usually acknowledged or noticed. Some business owners, especially in the beginning phase, lose their way when they start thinking of people as part of a target market or leads or prospects. What they are really talking about are people. The best way to connect to people is to build relationships with them. This can be done by looking for commonalities.

The pitch can be viewed as a form of marketing too. Marketing is a form of relating. It finds a way to relate to an aspect of people's senses. Good marketing attempts to relate to an audience in a way that will draw them to something. Your pitch is what I call Verbal Marketing. Verbal Marketing is finding ways to relate to an audience in order to draw and attract them to your product, service or business idea. By pointing out value.

When you pitch, finding ways to relate your product or service to the audience helps you build a relationship. That opens them up to receiving your information. Then, hopefully, it's just a matter of what works for them or not. Having this relationship with your business and knowing your stuff helps during the Q & A session. Everyone knows it's there and going to happen, but for some reason so many clam up, get tongue-tied, and either search endlessly for an answer, go into some random story that might lead to the answer or say something silly with a laugh hoping others laugh too.

Only the joke isn't funny and it just shows that you don't know the answer. And the story is a way of evading the information you don't have. Both of these can be avoided by knowing your stuff. That's having the best relationship you can have with your business.

When presenting a pitch or even standing on line at a coffee shop and having that notorious two-minute situation to describe what, why, and how, the key elements of your business, you still need to build a relationship; you need to connect. The way you share the information is very important.

In general people, want to be considered, appreciated, valued, heard, and thought of. Finding value and sharing that value is a lot better than trying to sell someone something. Even if they wanted or needed what you were offering, I promise you that most of the time they would seek it elsewhere if you try to sell them on it. Instead, have an authentic relationship and find a way to relate to their needs, wants, and concerns.

This is where the whole idea of solving a problem is important. You can use this to relate to how you can solve a problem or provide a solution. How can your whatchamacallit help them or someone they know? This is an easy way of connecting through commonalities, interests, and concerns.

It is best for you to have a relationship with and know your business while making an effort to relate to the audience when pitching. They will get that you understand your business and you will have a greater chance at getting what you want. It might seem that I'm hammering this idea in, but the truth is you have no idea how many company owners, salespeople, or team members of both already established and start-up businesses don't know what they really do or why they do it.

I have seen plenty of start-ups where the team members, and quite often the idea creators, have no clue what their product or service really is. It's mostly expected in the beginning stages of a start-up, but after several months, this should not be an issue. The idea should be crystalized.

At the end of the day, relationships are different for everyone, and yet they are the key to everything. The results in anything are all based on how we relate. Start by observing how you handle and deal with relationships in your life, even those moments with yourself and your business. How do you see things and how do you interpret them and how do you handle them? What are you thinking and feeling? Be honest, and then see where and how your outlook can be adjusted for the greater cause. Find ways to relate to people better and use the idea of common ground. Find ways to better relate the information you are communicating, and that will make your pitch more inviting.

Take advantage of every opportunity to practice your communication skills so that when important occasions arise, you will have the gift, the style, the sharpness, the clarity, and the emotions to affect other people.

—Jim Rohn

Connection

All things are connected like the blood that unites us. We do not weave the web of life; we are merely a strand in it. Whatever we do to the web, we do to ourselves.

—Chief Seattle

Chapter 7
Connecting

Communication—the human connection—is the key to personal and career success.

—Paul J. Meyer

This chapter is very similar to the one on Relationship. However, there is a small difference that I believe can help. Connection is so much more than what I'm going to mention here. Yet for our purposes, I'm only going to reference one small aspect of it, and that is to help you not feel alone and feel more comfortable while pitching. It is a small way of overcoming stage fright, shyness in front of people or whatever makes you reluctant to pitch, speak publicly, or network conversationally.

Through my years working with people, presenting onstage and in front of people in various forums, I have seen that many people hesitate to speak through a variety of reasons ranging from being shy, having low self-esteem or lack of confidence to cultural upbringings and differences. The tools I have gained from years in the personal-development field, studying human behavior, and acting make it easy to work with these people and help them overcome their fear. Feeling less alone and more comfortable in your setting can help with these anxieties.

Connection means realizing that you are not alone in anything, and that brings a level of comfort. The quote by Chief Seattle before the start of this chapter illustrates that perfectly. Not only is there a connection to other people, you are connected to animals, plants, and even the air you breathe. If you don't believe this is so, that's fine. But at least consider the fact of our connection to each other.

When you connect to the audience, you won't feel alone, and you'll feel less afraid and anxious. You won't forget your pitch, repeatedly put your hands in and out of your pockets or pace around the stage. So how do you connect with the audience? You can do it without even saying a word. And then, as you start to speak, you create a stronger connection and feel increasingly comfortable. By then, you will have done such a great job that the audience will want to connect with you when it's over.

Here are a few ways to make that connection. Imagine you're at a party or event where you don't know anyone. The event isn't large enough to get lost in the crowd, like a trade show with hundreds or thousands of people; this is more like a seventy-five-ish person event. People notice you enough that you are not hidden by the masses. Usually what people do in this situation is hope to not be seen or noticed or wait for someone else to strike up a conversation.

Unfortunately, when pitching, you cannot escape or wait for others to start conversations. But one thing you can do is look for a point of familiarity, such as a friendly smile, a business colleague, or a friend. This will keep you from being overwhelmed by the other people who are there. As you feel more and more comfortable, you will settle into a general comfort with the entire audience.

If this doesn't work for you, here is another trick: be inviting. Take a breath and a moment to smile, scan the whole audience, and say hello, good morning, or good afternoon. Greet your audience! You'd be amazed at how powerful this is.

Consider that the audience doesn't know you either. That alone should make you feel more comfortable and at least on equal ground. They don't know if you're going to throw knives, spit fire, yell at them, or speak like a mouse. Offering a simple greeting has an amazing effect on their receptivity. Just think how you would feel. This also does a great deal to boost your own confidence, your own comfort level, and your own energy. Quite simply, it lets guards down—yours and theirs.

The energy of the connection is like a current running through everything. You can pick it up and feel the current or disconnect yourself from it—the choice is yours. You also have a choice to affect the current by the way you act out and demand response. This thread of connectivity is a key to relationships, connection, and success in life and business.

However difficult life may seem, there is always something you can do and succeed at.

—Stephen Hawking

Turbocharge your Pitch

Be so good they can't ignore you.
—Steve Martin

Chapter 8
Pitching on Steroids

If your presence doesn't make an impact, your absence won't make a difference

---

Let's turbocharge your pitch. I'm going to suggest some points that can make your pitch more noticeable, professional, and memorable. These include appearance, attitude, and energy/presence.

First, let's put the pitch into perspective. We all know it's a business proposition of sorts. You're either looking for funding, customers, or team members—the three common areas of interest when pitching. At first, you need to know who you are pitching for. The audience matters, especially with content (what) and context (how).

A pitch is a presentation, and presentations can be given in a multitude of ways. Commonly, there is the dull corporate suit-and-tie stiff rendering with the standard PowerPoint slide show of charts and graphs. At the opposite end of the scale is the overboard high-energy, dressed to impress, loud and usually youngish new entrepreneur. Somewhere in the middle is the common Joe who is dressed casual and has a simple nature about him, hoping he gets it right.

The trick is to identify with the personality that is yours now. It doesn't have to be one of those mentioned above—it's a sliding scale. Where on the scale do you fit? Adjust the scale to identify your character depiction as it is now and as you present your pitch. Be honest.

Once you've decided what most closely represents your character in the presentation, we're going to change it. *Oh, no—what? I'm not changing, that's who I am, change to what?* Don't worry—you are actually going to fuel who you really are, only with a more suitable presence to get the job done. Remember, authenticity is key and highly valuable.

Let's face it: you are basically on the job interview of your life. If you want your listeners to take you seriously, you have to take them seriously and show them you care. Would you wear your pajamas to a business meeting? How about be tired and yawning or unprepared with details and information, stumbling over content?

Put things into perspective and consider that all things are relative. If you're giving a pitch and want to be taken seriously and respected, why not represent yourself as such? People like to work with other people who have a friendly, outgoing, and charismatic personality.

There is also the question of, are you the right person for the job? If you refuse to be the face or convincing personality that represents your business, then step aside. Usually, your company is made of a few team members—at least two in the beginning phase. Don't draw straws; identify the best person for the job and hope that person has a strong enough why and will step up.

My slogan is "Pitching with Presence, Pizzazz, and Professionalism." Let's look at it one piece at a time.

Presence

Sometimes you have to influence your attitude, personality, and disposition. One way to do so is through the clothes you wear. How you dress can affect your personality, attitude, and presence—for better or worse. Some days you feel "off," we get it. You're tired, overwhelmed, shy, uncomfortable, having bad hair day—you name it, that's life. However, the show must go on. When that happens, dress to impress *yourself.*

There have been studies, especially with school-age children, about the effect of the clothes students wear on their studies. The study basically says that their attire has an effect on their mental and emotional state, attention to study, and abilities. The more relaxed and casual their dress code was, the more relaxed and underachieving their work was. If they dressed smart and less casual, their attitude, attention, and study results improved. Generally, students in uniform were more productive and had overall better scores than those without. In addition, they also felt better about themselves.

I know this firsthand, having gone to schools that provided both options. Furthermore, I tested this theory at my workplace long after forgetting it from my school days. I worked in a generally relaxed and casual environment for many years. We basically wore whatever we wanted - jeans, sweats, t-shorts... I decided to change my dress code and dress smarter, with slacks, button-up shirts, and sometimes a short coat or suit without a tie. After getting over the initial few weeks of discomfort, with feelings of being overdressed among my colleagues, I noticed that my attitude, productivity, and attention to things changed for the better.

Mind you, I realize that this isn't true in all cases. Remember, I have a long history of being in the performing arts, and there is no dress code there. We all dress to express our inner artist. However, I did notice the shift when I became a teacher, trainer, and director. Those different roles required different personalities and a new outward expression of that character's personality in me.

After years of being an actor and having to dress the part for characters, you'd think I would know this. It is all the same thing. When you dress the part, you play it better and more convincingly. Sometimes you have to influence your inner world to affect and influence your outer world, and vice versa, thus helping to get the job done.

When you are presenting, you want to represent feeling good about yourself and what you are doing. You want to show that you're proud and interested in being involved with this idea. Show your audience that. If you're not feeling it that day, dress up for it. I believe that you should dress comfortably yet professionally—smart yet fun and friendly. Dress for success, show the world you are ready.

I can't say specifically what that is, because it is different for everyone. If you tune into your own true compass, you'll figure it out. For example, with considered exceptions: no jeans with holes, no sloppy shirts hanging out, no sneakers, use an iron and comb your hair. Get some sleep the night before. Eat for energy.

There is a marginal exception. If you're introducing a new skateboard or a pop culture product, service, or concept, dressing in jeans, Vans, and a T-shirt could work for you. However, it depends on the arena, platform, and environment, and to whom you're pitching. Which brings us to the next aspect.

Professionalism

Know your audience. Your approach, dress code, attitude, and content depend on who you're pitching to. I mentioned in earlier chapters the need to be authentic. Being authentic doesn't mean you can't still have an attitude, clothing or personality... adjustment.

If you're usually high-strung, wired, loud, and a really big expressive person, you might have to tone down and contain some of that while fund pitching. Knowing your audience is a part of the role you're to play as much as the information you're offering them. You can still be authentic, only now you're regulating the external representation of that authenticity to them.

For example: just because you are mad at somebody doesn't mean you have to yell and shout. Your frustration, anger, and how you are feeling can be expressed in a calm and controlled manner. The same is true for states of affection. You don't need to wildly throw your arms around somebody or kiss him or her ferociously in order to show affection. Also, you want to influence the situation, not be controlled by it or try to control it. You have the upper hand based on how and what you represent and present. Use this to your advantage.

Influencing your audience also means working them. You work your audience by relating to them. One way to do that is give them what they want in order to influence the higher probability of getting what you want. Language is a huge part of this. The aspect of professionalism is how your inner world is reflected on the outside. Be mindful of yourself and the way you express. That also means no cursing. It's a sure sign of a lack of self-control and not caring about what might offend others. Remember, you're not popular enough to get away with antics—although joking around intentionally isn't necessarily bad.

Pizzazz

Okay, so we have a basis for the professionalism and the presence, dealing with how your inner and outer worlds affect each other. Now let's put them together onstage with pizzazz. That's putting life and character into your presentation.

I already mentioned that tons of pitches are delivered with a dull and unenthusiastic energy. If that's your personality or the effect of your lack of interest for doing the pitch, that's fine. Get somebody who can put some life into it and cares or find a way to do it yourself.

It's not only about being excited, even a little. It's also about being creative, finding a way to present information that leaves a mark on the audience's brain. You want to make an impression on your potential investors, customers, and team members.

When I say to be excited or put life into the pitch, I don't mean to run around yelling and jumping. That's overkill, and there's plenty of that out there. Those presenters get unimpressed looks. That's too much. It's overacting, being the class clown, and looking for attention. When I say demand attention, I simply mean to show some enthusiasm. Make it seem that you want to be talking about your idea, product, or service—especially if it's your brainchild.

Another way to get geared up is to get inspired. If your feeling down, tired, whatever it might be, that's fine. However, that low energy won't do your presentation justice. If you know you're in that mood, use influences to adjust it. And I mean healthy ones. Listen to music, talk to a supportive friend, or read inspiring quotes. The music doesn't even have to be your kind, just something that gets you motivated. When considering music, look at the lyrics, not just the melody, rhythm, or tempo—although catchy tunes really help even if the words aren't right.

It may be something you listen to right before going out and may be just a few lines can do it for you. For instance: Eminem has a song called "Not Afraid." The title alone is inspiring. However, the lyrics or song might not fit your taste of music. Nonetheless, there are some words in the song that are pretty powerful.

Other suggestions include K'naan's "Better," Katy Perry's "Firework," and Survivor's "Eye of the Tiger." There is a whole album by Paul Hoffman called "Success Song." It's a good buy. It's not a high energy pump-you-up type, but it is inspirational.

It doesn't matter if it's rock and roll, religious/spiritual, pop—it's fine as long as it works for you. There are also inspirational quotes available online and in bookstores. Heck, you can even have a quote show up on your smartphone daily. BrainyQuote has a good website and phone app.

Now Get Out There and Break a Leg

Break a leg is a theatrical term that means good luck. It has no direct meaning, but the best I have seen is when one bends a knee to pick up the coins or flowers thrown on stage for a job well done or to bow/curtsy. I will leave you with one last quote (okay, maybe two).

Fun is good.—Dr. Seuss

Think left and think right and think low and think high. Oh, the thinks you can think up if only you try!
                          —Dr. Seuss

Afterword

Thank you for purchasing this book. If you received it from me or at a promotional venue, congrats. You've received something that can change your business and personal life alike. I want you to succeed in all aspects of your life, and because you are holding this book, you are closer to that goal. You have access to a free consultation on the evaluation of your pitch. All you have to do is go to the DADiNardi website, Www.DADiNardi.Com to the contact page; fill in the contact request form; and mention this note in the book. I am also available for services: Pitch Development, Pitch Presentation Training, Sales/ Marketing Communication Training and Pitch/Sales Presentations and Success Mindset Development.

Success is about taking action, and taking action is about fulfilling desires, wants, wishes, and dreams. Your dreams are worth pursuing no matter how small or large. There is no reason why anyone should not have the life he or she wants. I believe that we all have a piece of the puzzle that offers each of us a way to help others fulfill their dreams and life desires. I hope that this is a piece for your puzzle.

I believe it is a gift to offer value. Any time you learn something, share it! You'd be amazed at what happens next. I hope that you received something that can help you on your journey, whether in business or your personal life. And if you did—share it.

'Write with Passion, Act with Authenticity, Direct with S.M.A.R.T Goals and Produce with Gratitude'

About the Author

I started my journey as an actor and then eventually studied the other theatrical attributes of writing, directing and producing. In the beginning it was a hobby and over time became a more serious endeavor. I wanted to get to a level that I could leave the family business and ultimately have acting as my career path. However, acting had lead me to a more personal development life style which lead to the study of various spiritual practices around the globe from Buddhism, Hinduism, Metaphysics/ Holistic and Native American beliefs.

Not so focused on leaving the family business anymore, my personal development endeavors became more of my focus. I stayed to help grow and develop our business for several more years. Which open the doors to studying and understanding more about sales, marketing, stage selling and; what I call, audience/verbal marketing.

Things had come to a point in my life where I was tired of traditional business, and even though I tried my hand at several other personal business adventure it was time to find and focus on something I really liked. My wife and I decided to move the family to Europe. So, we packed ourselves and our two children up and moved to Finland.

This is where I had the opportunity to write the book I had always wanted to write. However, when in Finland I had discovered an entirely new culture, not only in species but in business as well. This propelled me in another direction. I had taken my idea I formulated for my original book idea and applied it to this book and the Start-up environment.

With my diverse back ground in the theater arts, business and personal development I am a shoe in for developing pitches, presentation and sales skills training. I developed a program uniquely based on my assorted experiences and compiled this book in hopes to offer a different and more efficient perspective on the pitch, presentations, sales and verbal marketing experience.

I use my stage skills as an asset for presentation training and business skills for pitch development and my character/human behavioral training for verbal marketing communication training. Combined, creates a powerful training program for stage presence, sales closing and company, product and service representation. Advising people how to communicate better, find ways to relate better and create situations that make selling easier instead of creating a feeling of having to sell something. Using the idea of relating as a primary point of interest. Relating to a person that is a potential customer, relating to an audience, and relating to a company, product or service.

When people are more confident and willing they are more efficient and capable.

Pitch Deck

- Introduction: "Hello, I am [name]." "We are [company name]."
- Product name and logo: Tagline is optional but favorable.
- Story: How the problem came to be noticed and your personal relationship to it
- What **problem** is it solving?
- What can it do or how can it **fix the problem**?
- Introduce product or service
- Identify target market and opportunities
- Competition: Why/how are you better/different from the competition? What's your edge?
- Marketing/sales: present and future - How and what are you doing to sell/market?
- Financial situation: projected revenue plan, how much you're looking for (if anything)
- Goals: future growth, products, services— one-, three-, and five-year forecast
- Team: Names, position, "important" credentials (for words or less)
- Why this is important to you? (*Optional*: wrap-up in less than six words)

Printed in the United States
By Bookmasters